Preschool Teachers

Teaching Basic Concepts

By Barbara F. Backer

Illustrated by Priscilla Burris

Warren Publishing House
A Division of Frank Schaffer Publications
Torrance, California

Managing Editor: Kathleen Cubley
Editor: Susan Hodges
Contributing Editors: Gayle Bittinger, Elizabeth McKinnon, Jean Warren
Copyeditor: Kris Fulsaas
Proofreader: Mae Rhodes
Editorial Assistant: Durby Peterson
Graphic Designer: Sarah Ness
Graphic Designer (cover): Brenda Mann Harrison
Layout Artist: Gordon Frazier
Production Managers: Jo Anna Haffner, Melody Olney

ISBN: 1-57029-098-9

Printed in the United States of America
Published by Warren Publishing House
    Editorial Office: P.O. Box 2250
                        Everett, WA 98203
    Sales Office: 23740 Hawthorne Blvd.
                        Torrance, CA 90505

20 19 18 17 16 15 14 13 12 11 10 9 8 7 6 5 4 3 2 1

Contents

Numbers

1 Numbers are everywhere, and opportunities for learning math concepts surround us. Make counting a part of every day. Count the steps as you go up and down, the doors you pass through, the number of stirs or shakes in cooking, and the number of berries you put in the pancakes. How many crayons will you use? Watch as your children's interest in numbers grows.

2 Fill your classroom with materials that support mathematical learning. In addition to commercial manipulatives and number lines, include measuring cups, clocks, thermometers, and rulers for measuring; and buttons, bolts, dried beans, and egg cartons for counting and sorting.

3 Use mathematical terms in your conversations with your children. "You have the square block and Jasmine has the rectangle. The red crayon is longer than the blue. Sydney is first in line. Eric is second. Patrick is last."

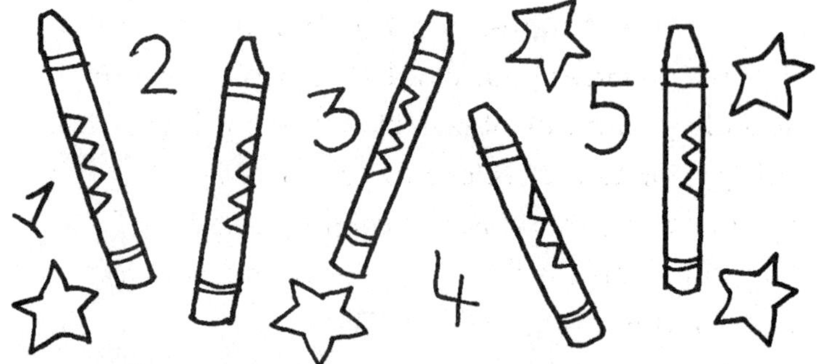

4 Invite your children to make a cooperative number book for each number you study. Each child contributes a page to the book. He or she decides which picture to make. For a *Three* book, a child might draw (or paste on) three rainbows, three dinosaurs, or three swings. Compile the drawings and add a construction paper cover. Place the *Three* book in your group's reading area.

5 Combine counting and singing in the following game. Put a long piece of tape on the floor to make a line. Choose one of your children to stand on the line, and sing the following song as a group. At the end of each verse, let the last child choose another child to join him or her on the line. Continue adding children, then count backward as one child at a time leaves the line.

Sung to: "The Farmer in the Dell"

One child on the line.
One child on the line.
Heigh ho, the derry-oh,
One child on the line.

Additional verses: Two children on the line; three children; etc.

Barbara Backer

6 Make simple number games from die-cut paper shapes (available at parent-teacher stores). Write a different numeral on each of eight shapes. Have your children place the corresponding number of objects on each shape. Try using shapes that relate to your learning themes. For instance, the children might put plastic-foam "peanuts" on elephant shapes or feathers on bird shapes.

7 Books about mathematical concepts show children that numbers are a part of everyday life. Include counting books, simple cookbooks, advertising circulars, and other number books in your language center.

8 To help your children practice counting, make a gameboard by laying out a pathway of stickers on a 12-by-18-inch piece of posterboard. Mark the starting place and the finish. For older children, include one or two "shortcuts" along the way, as shown in the illustration. The children roll a die and move colored bottle caps the number of spaces indicated.

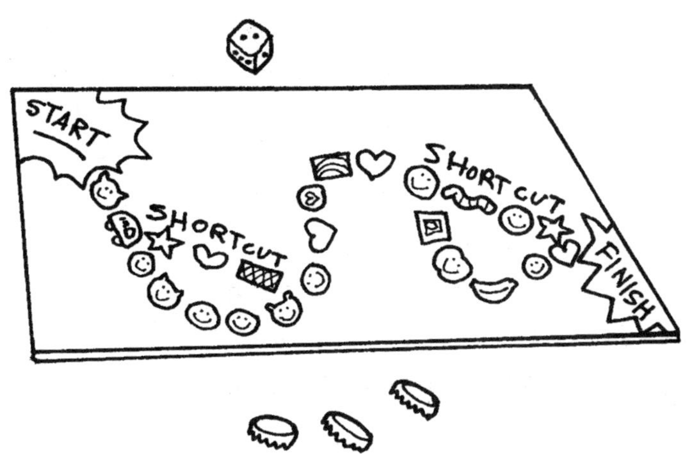

9 Turn shoeboxes on their sides to form bear caves, and place a numeral on the top of each cave. Let your children count out plastic teddy bear counters and put the correct number in each cave.

10 Your children can practice counting and writing when they "take inventory" of your room. Make a set of laminated inventory cards. Each card has pictures of five or six classroom items (table, hat, puppet) and a space for recording the number with a wipe off crayon. Draw the pictures or cut them out of catalogs. Remember to include pictures where the correct answer is zero (hippopotamus, birdhouse, bathtub).

Colors

1 Early in the school year, combine color learning with teaching your children where objects belong in your room. Gather a basket full of learning items of the same color. During large group, have your children take turns returning the items to their proper places. Encourage them to help each other.

2 Play a singing game about colors. Put colored paper circles in a hat or a sock. In turn, have each of your children pull out a circle and show the color. All the children then sing about this color. Make several circles of each color, and make more circles than there are children.

Sung to: "Mary Had a Little Lamb"

Rudy found a color
On a shape that's round.
Rudy found a color,
And red is what he found.

Repeat, substituting the name of one of one of your children for *Rudy*, and the name of the color he or she finds for *red*.

Barbara Backer

3 Match real items to make a color-matching game. Assemble a box of disposable plates, cups, and napkins in various colors. Have your children make sets of matching items.

4 To make a fun color-matching game for the winter months, cut snowman shapes and hats from heavy paper. Draw buttons on each snowman, giving each snowman a different color. Color hats to match the buttons. Have your children match the snowman and hat shapes.

8 Make a book about yellow. Have each of your children contribute a page, drawing what he or she wishes and using mostly yellow in the picture. Label each picture: yellow car, yellow butterfly, yellow ring, and so on. Make a book for each color you study.

9 Have your children help brainstorm a list of possible snacks that match the color you are studying. Red snacks might include spaghetti, pizza, apples, and tomato soup. Select one to serve the next day.

10 Make a color-matching game with index cards and large vinyl-coated paper clips. Using markers that match the paper clip colors, draw a colored stripe on each index card. Make a card to match each clip. To play the game, have your children slide clips onto matching cards.

5 Help your children focus on color with this activity. Cut two 4-inch squares of various fabrics. Have your children match the pairs. (Be careful when cutting plaids or large patterns, so the squares actually match.)

6 Play Color Tag outside. The leader calls out a color, and all your children wearing that color become "It," chasing friends who are not wearing the color. When the leader calls out a new color, the children wearing that color become "It."

7 Let your children discover what happens when they combine colors. Put out a variety of tempera paints, spoons, and jar lids. Have the children mix spoonfuls of color in their jar lids for use at the easel. Begin with two colors, then add more as the year progresses.

Shapes

1 Children learn with their whole bodies. Show them how to use their bodies to make shapes. Arrange three of your children on the floor so their bodies form a triangle. Each child's head touches the feet of another child. Remaining children gather around and count the sides (chests) and corners (heads) of the shape. Later, help children form a square, a circle, or a rectangle.

2 Cut large geometric shapes from appliance boxes. Cut out the center of each shape, yielding a large frame and a smaller solid shape. Place the shapes flat on the floor. Lean the frames against walls and furniture, or suspend them from the ceiling so they just touch the floor. Direct your children to move over, under, around, beside, or through the shapes and frames.

3 Display pictures of shapes. Challenge your children to make similar shapes with pipe cleaners.

4 Arrange paper shapes on the floor and have your children outline them with unit blocks. Remove the paper to reveal the shape's outline. Repeat using pencils, unit cubes, popsicle sticks, buttons, or other objects.

5 Children enjoy making books. Ask your children to make books about triangles. On each page, they can draw or glue a triangle in a different color. Label the pages: red triangle, blue triangle, green triangle. Make similar books for each shape you study.

6 Divide an open file folder into three columns. Across the top draw a triangle, a rectangle, and a circle. Cut index cards in half. On every card draw a picture of an object that includes a basic shape. Have one of your children look at the picture and place it on the folder under the matching shape.

Variation: Instead of index cards, use photographs of real items for this game.

7 Cut geometric shapes from poster-board. Place several pairs of these in a bag. Have your children take turns reaching into the bag and feeling for the shape you request. Vary the game according to each child's abilities: you might ask a child to find a specific shape, such as a square, or two shapes that are the same. With practice, children can tell each other what to pull from the bag.

8 Cut shapes from 4-inch squares of paper, using red for triangles, blue for circles, and yellow for squares (or rectangles). Have your children search the room for shapes: square book, round mixing bowl, triangular coat hanger. Have them put paper shapes near the corresponding items. Write the name of the item on its corresponding precut shape, one item per shape. Help the children graph the shapes. Which one is the most common?

9 Make a set of paper shapes, including at least one example of each shape your children know. Make as many shapes as you have children, plus a few extra. Gather your children in a circle and give each one a paper shape. Then sing the following song, holding up a different paper shape for each verse. Have the children whose shapes match yours hold up their shapes. When every child has held up his or her shape, have the children trade shapes and begin the game again.

Sung to: "The ABC Song"

I have a triangle, look and see.
If you have a triangle, show it to me.

Barbara Backer

10 Encourage family involvement in learning by making a take-home learning game for your children. Cut an assortment of shapes out of different colors of construction paper. Cover each shape with clear self-stick paper for durability. The children can use the shapes to make pictures, or they can sort them according to shape or color. Let each child in turn take the game home for a few days.

Letters

1 Encourage your children to form letters with modeling dough. Make letter cards by writing one letter on each of 26 index cards. Laminate the cards. Have the children roll modeling dough snakes and arrange the snakes along the letters' outlines.

2 Select four or five plastic letters that have very different shapes, like S, E, R, O, and Y. Place each inside a stretch sock. Make a letter card to match each letter. Have your children feel the plastic letters through the socks and place each sock on the matching letter card. As the children become more confident, add a few more letters and socks. Change letters and letter cards often.

3 Collect a variety of kinds of letters—cardboard, wooden, magnetic, printed on paper, printed on colored index cards, written with white glue on index cards, cut from sandpaper and glued to cardboard, or cut from advertising and glued to index cards.

4 Use a black marker and write a different letter on each of 26 index cards. Place five of these in a basket. Add the same letters in wooden, magnetic, and sandpaper letters. Challenge your children to match letters to the letter cards. Change the letters in the basket from time to time.

5 Young children love to hunt for treasure. Give each of your children a letter shape and have him or her find matching letters somewhere in the room. They can look on calendars; on posters; in books, catalogs and magazines; in phone books; and in many other places.

8 Contact your local school district to find out what style of handwriting (e.g., D'Nealian, Zaner-Bloser, Modern) is taught in kindergarten. Teach your children how to write their name in that style.

9 Write each child's name on an index card, and place the cards in the art center. Children who are ready will copy their names onto their artwork. Place more cards in the language center where the children can copy their own and each other's names.

10 Provide a generous supply of writing materials for your children to use as they experiment with print. Chubby pencils, pens, and crayons are easier for little hands to grip. Wrap rubber bands or masking tape around the ends of pencils for ease in writing.

6 Display a variety of alphabet books in your group's reading area. Read them often, and add new ones regularly. Older children can make their own ABC books. Give each of your children a book with 26 pages and a letter of the alphabet on each page. Over a period of weeks, have the child draw a picture to go with the letter on each page.

7 Have your children use their bodies to form letter shapes on the floor. How many children does it take to make an *I*? An *N*?

Opposites

1 Children learn about opposites by experiencing them. Have a tasting party to taste and identify things that are sweet or sour. Suggestions include graham crackers, apple juice, and jelly; lemon juice, dill pickles, and tart apples.

2 For another experience, have your children stretch up high to become as tall as possible, then stoop very low to become short. Next, tell the children to spread their arms and legs to make themselves very wide, then have them make themselves as narrow as possible.

3 Have your children help you collect items to illustrate large and small. Display the items and compare their sizes.

4 Play Simon Says using opposite concepts: high and low, big and little, near and far.

5 Help your children collect pictures and real items to make a mural of opposites. You might include such items as a new and an old shoelace, a laundry detergent advertisement featuring a clean shirt and a dirty one, pictures of a happy person and a sad one, and pictures of a hot bowl of soup and a cold iced drink.

6 Have your children pose for pictures that illustrate opposites: Justin near and Justin far; the wagon full of children, the wagon empty; the children going up the steps, the same children coming down. Put these pictures side by side in a photo album or a group-made book.

7 Play Follow the Leader, announcing where you are going as you move along: Over the balance beam and under the jungle gym, or up the steps and down the slide.

8 Bring in a filled hot water bottle and an ice bag. Pass them around and let your children feel them and discuss them. Make lists of things that are hot and things that are cold.

9 Collect items to illustrate narrow and wide: a regular crayon and a jumbo crayon, or fabric with pinstripes and fabric with wide stripes. Have your children put narrow items together on a long, narrow rectangle of paper and wide items together on a wider paper rectangle.

10 Have your children gather a variety of objects. Now have the children sort them into two categories, hard and soft. Help your children think of other categories by which to sort the items.

Matching

Use this matching activity at the beginning of the year to help your children learn where items are in the room. Take photos of items in your room such as a block, a pencil, a crayon, scissors, a doll's shoe, and a paintbrush. During circle time, give a photo to each child. Challenge the children to find the matching items. Have them exchange photos so they put away a different item, learning where it goes.

Save decorated cups and napkins from birthday and holiday parties throughout the year. Bring others from fast food restaurants. Place all of these in a box for a matching game.

Cut two squares from several patterns of wrapping paper. Glue these on squares of cardboard to make a matching game. To play, spread half the squares on the floor. Place the matching squares in a hat. In turn, let each of your children choose a square from the hat and find its match on the floor.

Take pictures of the fronts and backs of familiar items and people: a doll, a chair, a puppet, your program's van, the teacher, a child. Have your children find the matching pairs.

Have each of your children (and each teacher) remove one shoe and put it in the middle of the circle. One at a time, give the children a chance to select a shoe and return it to its owner.

6 Make a game that requires your children to match real items to their outlines. On posterboard, trace around several spoons of various sizes, assorted kitchen gadgets, a large paper clip, and other familiar items. Store the gameboard and the items in a box.

7 Videotape your children as they arrive in your classroom, but do not show their heads or faces. Later, show the video and see if the children can identify each other from the body pictures.

8 Ask your children to bring in their baby pictures. Display these and challenge the children to discover the identity of each "mystery baby."

9 Have dolls of different sizes in your room, and provide several sets of clothes for each doll. Children learn reasoning skills as they dress the dolls, matching correct clothes to dolls of different sizes.

10 Can your children match parts of items to the whole item? Display yarn and a crocheted potholder or sweater, a newspaper picture and a section of the newspaper, a telephone book page and a telephone book, a doll shoe and a doll. Challenge the children to think of other possibilities.

Classifying

1 Food activities capture children's attention. Make sorting a part of snacktime. Make a sorting placemat for each of your children by drawing lines to divide a piece of paper into four parts. Glue a circle onto one section and a square, a rectangle, and a triangle onto remaining sections. Cover each with a sheet of plastic wrap before using. Serve each child a handful of crackers in assorted shapes, and let the child sort the crackers on his or her sorting mat.

2 Give each of your children a bottom section of an egg carton and a small plastic bag containing a mixture of raisins, square cereal pieces, O-shaped cereal, dried banana slices, and sunflower seeds. Have the children sort the items into the egg carton cups. Discuss the results. "Juan put all of the dried fruit together. Trina put all of the brown things together." Have them dump everything into the bag and sort items a new way, then invite them to eat their work!

3 Make a "Family Game." Make four columns on a piece of posterboard. Glue a catalog picture of a person at the top of each column—a dad, a mom, a preschool child, and an infant. Make game cards by gluing catalog pictures onto individual index cards. Choose items that would be used by one or more of the people— a lamp, a blender, a crib, a tricycle, a soccer ball, a lawnmower, a purse, etc. Laminate the cards. To play the game, have one of your children give each item to the family member he or she thinks is most appropriate. Accept all responses.

4 Gather empty film canisters (from a photo processing lab) and a variety of scented stickers, four of each scent. Stick each sticker on the lid of a canister. Have your children scratch and sniff the stickers, then put matching canisters together in groups. Surprisingly, children don't sort the stickers by looking at them.

5 Invite a small group of your children to sit in a circle. Roll a ball from one person to another and discuss rolling. Then give each child a basket of small items. Include things that roll (cars, pompons, crayons) and things that do not roll (blocks, magnets, playing cards). Challenge the children to test their items and divide them into two categories: things that roll and things that do not.

6 Play a similar game with magnets. Give each child in your small group a basket containing a magnet and an assortment of items. Include some magnetic items (paper clips, screws) and some nonmagnetic ones (plastic spoons, blocks). Also include items that have magnetic parts (spring-type clothespins, pencils with metal tops.) Give your children time to explore the items and discover that some stick to the magnets. Then have them test each item and sort them into two categories: things that stick to a magnet and things that do not.

7 Make a classifying game based on familiar items. Cut pictures of classroom equipment or housewares from old catalogs. Mount each picture on an index card. Set out the cards and let your children classify the pictures according to their location in the classroom or home.

8 During circle time, call up your children one at a time and sort them into groups. At first tell the children the categories and let them help you decide where each child belongs. Suggested categories: eye color, boy or girl, children wearing blue and children not wearing blue. Next, call the children one at a time and classify them silently. Can the children guess the categories? As the children gain skill, let them take turns directing the classifying.

9 Often children sort items into groups according to someone else's directions: "Put the round ones here and the square ones there." After they have had many experiences doing that, provide your children with opportunities to determine their own categories (classification). Given a container of bottle caps, one child may make groups according to color, another according to size, another according to whether the caps are metal or plastic.

10 From two colors of construction paper, cut out large, medium-sized, and small shapes, including triangles, circles, and squares. Offer these to your children and watch to see if they sort by one, two, or three attributes—color, size, or shape. All responses are acceptable, and new skills will appear over time.

Spatial Relationships

1 Building a small sandwich for snack is a great way to learn about spatial relations. Offer cheese and crackers and sing this song about the finished product.

Sung to: "Down by the Station"

Take a square cracker,
Put it on the bottom,
Cheese in the middle,
And cracker on the top.
Take a big bite now
Of my cracker sandwich.
Crunch, crunch, yum, yum—
Now it's gone!

Barbara Backer

2 Ask your children, "Which is nearer, the trash can or the filing cabinet? The piano or the door?" The children can use different colors of yarn to measure the distances, then compare the lengths of yarn.

Challenge them to think of other ways to measure. They may try walking heel to toe to the object, snapping together unit cubes, or lining up index cards. Try as many as possible. Discuss why some are better than others. When Erica (with big feet) and Alana (with little feet) walk heel to toe to the door, they have different numbers of steps. Why?

3 Movement activities help children become aware of the space occupied by their bodies. They discover that they need more space for running and jumping than for walking and hopping. Help your children discover that hopping is an up-and-down motion, while jumping a distance is a forward motion. Challenge the children to find new ways of moving forward, backward, sideways, and up and down.

4 Take photographs that show spatial relations. Place them in a photo album and label them: "Luis is over Charlie and under Laquita. They are all on the jungle gym;" or "Jenny and Lakisha are beside the tree. Sarita is behind it." Place the photo album in your group's reading area.

8 Provide a variety of large boxes for your children to play with and play in as they explore volume. Ask, "How many children can fit in this box if they are standing? Sitting? How many stuffed animals can fit inside? How many blocks?"

9 Provide a variety of plastic jars and kitchenware containers that each have the same volume capacity but are different shapes. Ask your children if they are the same or if one will hold more. Have a child fill one to the rim with modeling dough. Then have him or her transfer the dough to another container. The children won't immediately understand that the containers hold the same amount. They'll think the modeling dough changed. Store these and similar containers with the modeling dough and keep more in the sand or water table for further experimentation.

5 If one center becomes too crowded with children, ask, "How can we make more room in this center?" Your children may suggest removing items, stacking items, moving shelves and other partitions, moving other furniture, and removing extra children. Discuss how and why different suggestions help or don't help solve the problem. Try all safe suggestions.

6 Have your children make items for a mural about the Three Billy Goats Gruff and the Troll. Label the mural: "The Troll is under the bridge. The biggest goat is on the bridge. Two goats are in the meadow."

10 Provide opportunities for your children to see things from a different perspective. Meet with a small group of children under a table. Discuss what you see from that perspective. Can the children identify their friends by what they see (legs and feet)?

7 Set out several small cardboard boxes. How many snap-together unit cubes do your children think these will hold? Have the children work in pairs to fill a box with unit cubes, then remove the cubes and snap them together. Compare the resulting stacks of cubes to compare the volume capacity of the boxes.

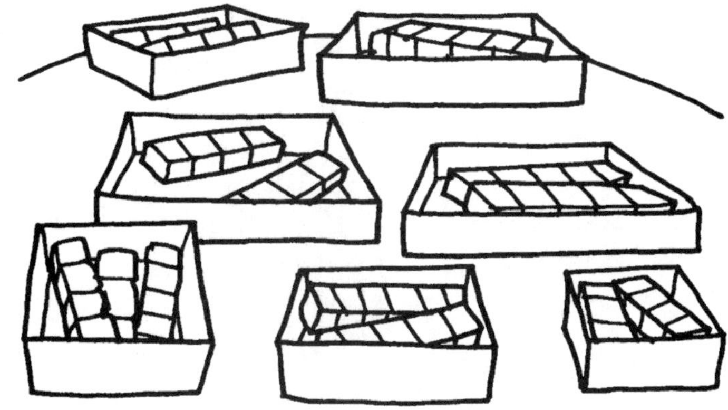

Sequencing and Seriation

1 Ordinal numbers tell the order of things. Your children practice using ordinal numbers when they recite the following fingerplay, pointing to fingers as they go. After they learn the words, five children at a time can act out the rhyme while the remaining children recite it.

> The first little frog went hop, hop, hop.
> The second little frog said,
> "Stop, stop, stop!"
> The third little frog stubbed his toe.
> The fourth little frog said,
> "Oh, oh, oh."
> The fifth little frog said,
> "I see some flies!"
> So the frogs ate dinner
> And winked their eyes.
> Ribbit! Ribbit! Ribbit! Ribbit! Ribbit!

Barbara Backer

2 Gather four identical cottage cheese (or similar opaque) containers. Fill the first three with varying amounts of salt. Leave the fourth empty. Glue lids on all containers. Have your children lift the containers, compare them, and arrange them in order by weight.

3 Make a sequencing game for each of your children using photographs of the child. Ask his or her parent to send in pictures of the child as an infant, and at ages one, two, and each year up to a current photo.

Photocopy the pictures. Mount the copies on cardboard, cut into separate cards and laminate. Have the child place the photos in order. The children will enjoy playing with one another's cards.

4 Photograph your group's daily activities—circle time, snack, outside play, etc. Show the pictures to your children and let them try to put them in sequence.

5 Take sequential photographs of your children's special projects. For instance, if your children make a mural, take snapshots of the blank paper, the paper with one item on it, with more items, and then the completed mural. Have your children place the photos in order.

6 Play Go Where I Go with your children outdoors. The first child touches an object (the slide). The second child touches the same object plus a second object (the slide, a tree). The third child touches the previous objects in order, plus a third. When a child misses, he or she becomes the first child as the game starts over.

7 Cut three pictures of the same item in three different sizes of items (three shirts, three cars, three W's) from magazines, catalogs, or newspapers. Ask your children to glue the pictures on construction paper from largest to smallest. As the children gain skill, use four or five pictures.

8 Find four identical yogurt containers with opaque lids. Place several nails in one, dried beans in another, salt in the third, and leave the last one empty. Glue the lids on the containers. Have your children shake the containers and place them in order from loudest to quietest. As the children gain skill, add other containers.

9 Children love to sing and they develop auditory memory and sequence skills as they sing songs with many verses. "On Top of Spaghetti" and "I Know an Old Lady" are two examples.

10 Play Move Like Me, Then Add Another with your children. In a circle, the first child makes a motion to music, and all follow along to the count of ten. The second child adds another motion, which the children follow to the count of ten; then they repeat the first motion ten times. Each succeeding child adds another motion until things become too confused. At that point, start again!

Cooperation and Sharing

1 Children learn the fun of working together when they make a "Cooperation Monster." At your children's eye level, hang a large piece of paper on a door or a wall. Begin the activity by drawing a head shape on the paper. Invite your children to work together to complete the monster, each adding a body part or other detail.

2 Making bulletin boards can be a cooperative venture. Decide on a topic like a garden or a football game, then discuss what you will need to create the scene. Let your children paint the background together. Then have them make the necessary components—flowers, bird feeder, and insects or a field, players, and goal posts. Ask each child, "What do you want to add next?" Take photographs at various steps along the way. These can later be used for a sequencing activity.

3 Send your children in pairs to the snack center, where each can make a snack for the other, or to the art center, where partners can make gifts for each other.

4 Divide your children into pairs and give each pair a grocery bag full of blocks. Let them decide what to build and work together to accomplish the task. Be aware that not all children are able to work this way. Support each child at his or her own level. A child who needs to work independently can be encouraged to build near his or her partner. "Janet is building a skyscraper. Could you make a parking garage?"

5 Pair your children or put them into groups of three or four to put together puzzles. The weaker puzzle builders learn from watching others' techniques. All have a feeling of accomplishment with the finished product.

6 Have your children verify one another's work when playing matching games. The checker benefits from working through to make certain the matches are correct and often stays behind to re-work the activity.

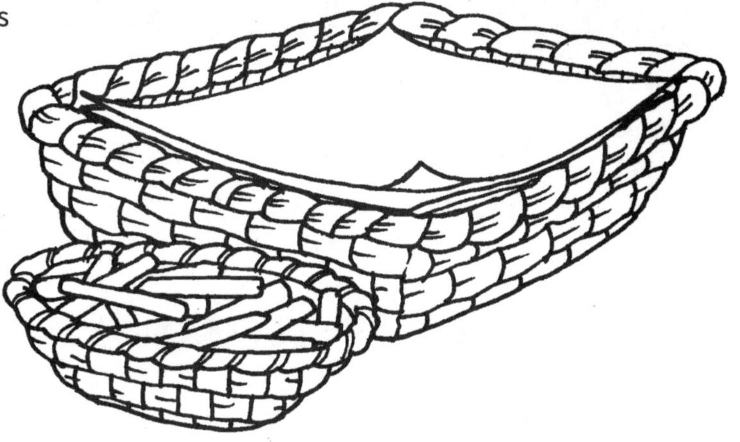

7 Older children enjoy cooperating to make a book of frightful monsters. Have your children sit at a table. Each child draws a head on his sheet of paper, then passes the drawing to the right. Each child adds eyes and passes the drawing to the right. Continue passing the papers as the children add noses, mouths (with or without teeth), bodies, arms, legs, and clothes. Compile all the drawings into a "Frightful Monsters" book and add it to the group's reading area.

8 When you play alphabet or number bingo, pair your children who are adept at letter or number recognition with the children who are not. Hold up the letter or number cards so the children can see the cards as you call them. Have the children work together to match letters or numbers and to cover the matches on their cards.

9 When your children are working at the art center, provide enough materials for each child, but place them all together so the children experience the feeling of sharing. For example, put art papers in one basket on the table and all crayons in another.

10 Call a local quilting society and ask a member to visit your program to show quilts, including one consisting of squares made by several quilters. Explain to your children that making a quilt can be a cooperative venture. Give each child a paper square to decorate with markers. Gather all of these and hang them side by side, top to bottom, to make a mural. Label the mural, "Cooperation Quilt."

Use Totline® Resources

When you need ideas for helping young children learn and grow, turn to Totline Publications. Our books are quality, classroom-tested resources for teachers, directors, daycare providers, parents, and others who work with children ages 2 to 6. The innovative ideas presented in our materials challenge and engage young children but need only minimal preparation and common, inexpensive materials. Totline Publications makes learning fun for everyone.